D1709384

TRUE STORIES OF

BY ARNOLD RINGSTAD

Published by The Child's World®
1980 Lookout Drive • Mankato, MN 56003-1705
800-599-READ • www.childsworld.com

Acknowledgments
The Child's World®: Mary Berendes, Publishing Director
Red Line Editorial: Editorial direction
The Design Lab: Design
Amnet: Production

Photographs © Matt Faber/PA Wire/Associated Press, cover
(center), 1 (center), 11; Michael Price/Thinkstock, back cover
(top), 3 (bottom), 13; Eric Isselee/Thinkstock, back cover
(bottom), 3 (top), 7, 23; Thinkstock, cover (top), cover (bottom
right), 1 (top), 1 (bottom right), 2–3, 17; Bettmann/Corbis, 4,
20; iStockphoto, 5 (top), 14; Manuel Balce Ceneta/AP
Images, 5 (bottom); Dmitry Lovetsky/AP Images, 6; Arne Dedert/
Picture-Alliance/DPA/AP Images, 9; Phelan M. Ebenhack/
AP Images, 12; Regis Duvignau/Reuters/Corbis, 15; Alan
Rogers/Casper Star-Tribune/AP Images, 16; Ed Andrieski/
AP Images, 19; PhotoDisc, 21

ISBN 9781626873612
LCCN 2014930700

Printed in the United States of America
Mankato, MN
July, 2014
PA02225

ABOUT THE AUTHOR

Arnold Ringstad lives in Minnesota. He wouldn't want his cat flying into space.

CONTENTS

ANIMALS AT WORK

Some animals have jobs to do. Just like people, they must train to learn how to do their jobs. Animals work with the police. They search for buried mushrooms. They even fly into space! Read on to learn more about these and other stories of animals at work.

Some animals work just like people do.

Helping Kids Learn

Some dogs help kids practice reading.

Some schools use dogs to help kids learn. Kids who have trouble reading read aloud to these dogs. It can be a great way to practice. One of the dogs' trainers said, "If they make a mistake, the dog isn't going to correct them. It's just going to listen and love every word they said."

Ross is one of these dogs. He is an Irish setter, a friendly dog with long hair. Ross works at schools in Maryland. He helps kids relax when they are reading. After reading for 30 minutes, kids get to play with Ross as a reward.

Working with Ross, kids quickly become better readers. One student improved his reading in just a few months. Ross helped him practice.

Ross listens while a student reads to him.

A Team of Cats

A Hermitage Museum
cat takes a cat nap.

Museums usually have many security guards. These workers walk through the rooms of museums. They make sure no one takes anything or damages the art. Most museum guards use radios to help them protect the art. But one special group of guards in Russia uses paws instead!

A group of cats work at the Hermitage Museum in St. Petersburg, Russia. The cats run through the museum and catch mice. They stop the mice before they can frighten museum visitors or damage artwork.

The cats do not go into rooms with artwork. Instead, they chase mice through the museum's back rooms, away from visitors. But the oldest cat, Vaska, figured out how to get into public areas. Vaska wanders through the amazing pieces of art at the Hermitage Museum. One museum worker said of Vaska, "He usually does it on Mondays, when the museum is closed to visitors."

The Hermitage Museum cats catch mice.

Keeping Crowds Safe

When large crowds of people gather, there is a risk of danger. Though unusual, people can get pushed around or knocked down. Others may get stepped on. People can get packed so close together it is hard to breathe. One job police have is keeping crowds safe. They sometimes get help from special animal workers: police horses.

Lara the police horse works in Frankfurt, Germany. She works with policeman Mario Hies to keep people safe. Police horses in Germany often work at sporting events. Big crowds of soccer fans get excited after games. It is up to Lara, other horses, and police officers to keep them safe.

In 2013, Lara and other police horses in Germany got new equipment for their jobs. Strong pieces of plastic protect their eyes. Leg protectors let them walk easily through large crowds. Ear protectors let them work safely without being scared by loud noises. Her new equipment will help Lara keep people safe.

Lara the police horse shows off her new eye protection.

Dog of the Millennium

Service dogs help people lead happy, fulfilling lives. Some help blind people get around. Others keep older people company. One special service dog became world famous. His name was Endal. He lived with Allen Parton. Parton is a military **veteran** from the United Kingdom.

After the Gulf War (1990-1991), Parton was badly injured. He had to use a wheelchair to get around. Parton also suffered from memory loss. He had trouble remembering family members. Endal helped Parton with daily tasks. The dog helped him answer the phone, send letters, and do many other things. He even saved Parton's life.

One day, Parton and Endal were crossing a street. A car hit Parton. He was knocked out of his wheelchair. Endal leaped into action. He moved Parton into a safe position. He covered his owner with a blanket. Then, he ran away to get help. The story of Endal's actions was in newspapers around the world. Some people even called him the "Dog of the **Millennium**."

Endal helped Parton mail letters.

Putting on a Show

Kayla the orca performs
with her trainer.

Cetaceans are mammals that live in the sea. Dolphins,
orcas, and other whales are all cetaceans. These animals
are very smart. They can be trained to do all kinds of tricks.

Some cetaceans living at marine parks are so well trained that they put on shows for people. An orca named Kayla is one of these cetaceans.

Kayla works at a marine park in Florida. She has also worked in Texas and Ohio. Kayla has been working for more than 20 years. Like all orcas, she is huge. Orcas can be more than 30 feet (9 m) long. Kayla weighs more than 5,000 pounds (2,270 kg). Despite their size, she and other orcas leap out of the water. They perform other tricks. They work closely with trainers to put on shows.

Kayla is one of the smartest whales at her park. She can make noises, spit water, and wave her fins. She can even do more than one of her tricks at once.

The Truffle Hunter

A truffle is a rare kind of mushroom. Many people love adding truffles to foods. But the mushrooms can be tough to find. They grow underground. Who do people turn to when they want to find truffles? They get help from hardworking pigs. One of them is named Magali.

Magali the pig works in France. This is where many truffles are found. Pigs have a great sense of smell. They use their noses to find the truffles. There is something else that makes pigs great for the job. Magali's owner said, "A pig will search all day, whereas a dog gets bored after a few

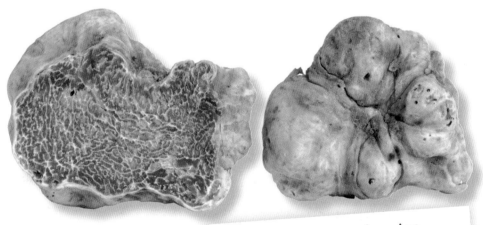

It takes time for pigs to sniff out truffles.

Magali hunts for truffles with her owner.

hours." However, pig owners must be careful. Pigs love the taste of truffles. Owners must grab the truffles before the pigs eat them.

The pigs can bring in a lot of money for their work. Just 2 pounds (1 kg) of truffles can sell for more than $1,000.

The Hunting Eagle

Scott Simpson with his
golden eagle, Maggie.

Millions of Americans enjoy hunting. They go out into
the wilderness. Some use guns to hunt. Others use bows
and arrows. But not many people use birds. One exception
is Scott Simpson. He goes hunting with his golden
eagle, Maggie.

Eagles are natural hunters. They have sharp eyesight. Eagles can spot prey from far away. They can fly faster than 40 miles per hour (64 kph). The birds have sharp **talons** for grabbing prey. Eagles hunt many animals, including fish, ducks, and mice.

Simpson and Maggie live in Wyoming. Simpson takes Maggie out to large, open fields. He lets her go. Then, Maggie flies into the air to hunt. She comes back with rabbits. The birds can be dangerous, so the government requires people to get licenses to hunt with eagles. Only about 60 people in the United States have these licenses. That makes Maggie an animal with an unusual job.

FUN FACT
Though they only weigh about 10 pounds (4.5 kg), golden eagles are very strong. Their talons can grip things 15 times tighter than a human hand can!

A Bomb-Sniffing Dog

Many dogs help save lives in the military. Their powerful sense of smell helps them find hidden bombs. One of these brave dogs is named Gina. She worked for the U.S. military during the Iraq War (2003–2011).

Battlefields can be loud and frightening places. In Iraq, Gina was often near explosions. After spending months at war, Gina returned home. But she was not the same. She became scared when entering buildings. She would hide from new people. Military **veterinarians** realized that she suffered from the same **mental health** problems that affect some soldiers.

Gina's handlers found ways to help her adjust. They took her on walks near people she knows. They played sounds she might hear in the military. This helped her get used to these noises again. Gina went back to work for the military, but only in the United States. Dog handlers think it is important to help the dogs feel better: "You can't really give up on them. They're your partner."

Gina sits with Staff Sergeant Chris Kench at an Air Force dog kennel.

Space Ape

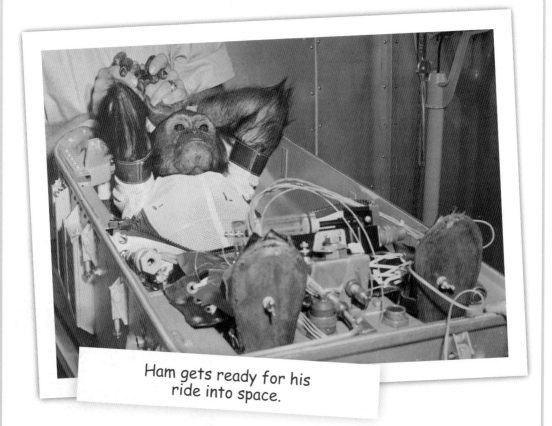

Ham gets ready for his ride into space.

In the 1960s, the United States and the Soviet Union built rockets to travel into space. However, these first rockets were unpredictable. They were not safe enough for people to ride in them. Governments turned to very special workers to test the rockets: monkeys and apes!

One of these workers was Ham the chimpanzee. Ham was the first chimpanzee to travel into space. He was just three years old when he made his trip. Ham launched into space on January 31, 1961. He flew on a rocket called the *Mercury Redstone*.

Ham went faster and higher than any chimp had gone before. He zoomed through space at 5,857 miles per hour (9,426 kph). He reached 157 miles (253 km) in **altitude**. Then, his spacecraft used a parachute to land softly in the sea back on Earth. Afterward, doctors checked him out. They found that Ham was healthy. Ham's mission helped prove it was safe to fly into space. The first people flew into space just a few months later.

FUN FACT
Many other kinds of animals have been sent into space. Mice, rats, and rabbits were some early passengers. In 1968, the Soviet Union sent turtles, worms, and flies to the moon and back.

altitude (AL-tuh-tood) Altitude is the height something is above the ground. Ham the chimpanzee reached a very high altitude.

cetaceans (set-AY-shunz) Cetaceans are mammals that live in the sea. Orcas are cetaceans.

mental health (MEN-tul helth) Mental health is the state of someone's mind, including emotions and thoughts. Gina's mental health suffered after she returned home from war.

millennium (muh-LEN-ee-um) A millennium is a period of 1,000 years. Endal was called the Dog of the Millennium.

service dogs (SUR-vis dogz) Service dogs are dogs that help people with daily tasks. Some service dogs guide blind people around cities.

talons (TAL-unz) Talons are bird claws. Eagles use talons to grasp their prey.

veteran (VE-tur-in) or (VE-trin) A veteran is someone who fought in a war. Endal's owner was a veteran.

veterinarians (VET-ur-in-AIR-ee-unz) Veterinarians are doctors who take care of animals. Veterinarians realized Gina suffered from mental health problems.

BOOKS

125 True Stories of Amazing Animals: Inspiring Tales of Animal Friendship and Four-Legged Heroes, Plus Crazy Animal Antics. Washington, DC: National Geographic, 2012.

Fretland VanVoorst, Jenny. *Seeing-Eye Dogs.* New York: Bearport, 2014.

Palika, Liz. *Animals at Work.* Hoboken, NJ: Wiley, 2009.

WEB SITES

Visit our Web site for links about animals at work: *childsworld.com/links*

Note to Parents, Teachers, and Librarians: We routinely verify our Web links to make sure they are safe and active sites. So encourage your readers to check them out!

INDEX